CINCINNATI BENGALS

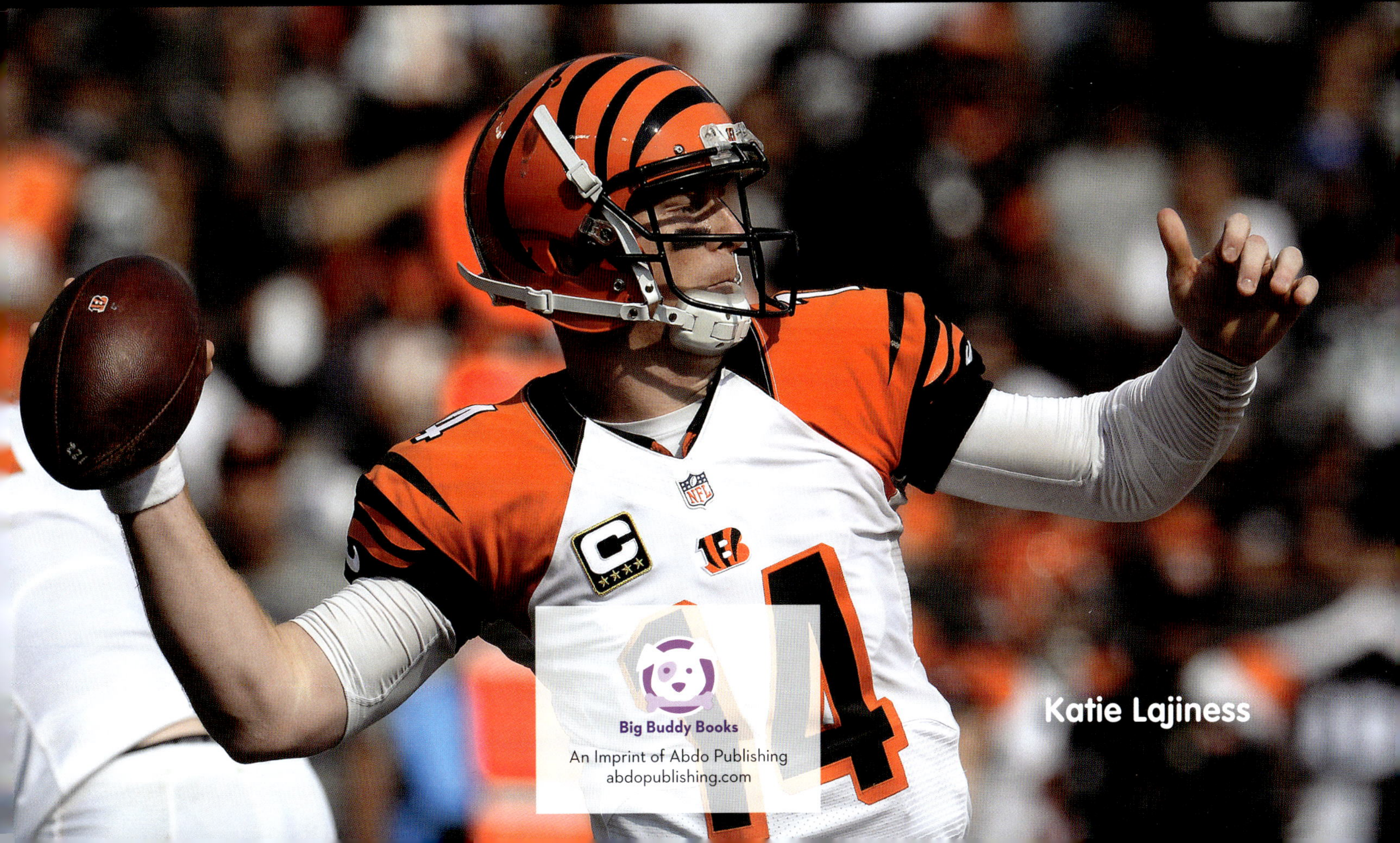

Katie Lajiness

Big Buddy Books
An Imprint of Abdo Publishing
abdopublishing.com

abdopublishing.com

Published by Abdo Publishing, a division of ABDO, PO Box 398166, Minneapolis, Minnesota 55439.

Printed in the United States of America, North Mankato, Minnesota.
092016
012017

Cover Photo: Tribune Content Agency LLC/Alamy Stock.
Interior Photos: ASSOCIATED PRESS.

Coordinating Series Editor: Tamara L. Britton
Graphic Design: Michelle Labatt, Taylor Higgins, Jenny Christensen

Publisher's Cataloging-in-Publication Data

Names: Lajiness, Katie, author.
Title: Cincinnati Bengals / by Katie Lajiness.
Description: Minneapolis, MN : Abdo Publishing, 2017. | Series: NFL's greatest teams | Includes bibliographical references and index.
Identifiers: LCCN 2016944874 | ISBN 9781680785319 (lib. bdg.) | ISBN 9781680798913 (ebook)
Subjects: LCSH: Cincinnati Bengals (Football team)--History--Juvenile literature.
Classification: DDC 796.332--dc23
LC record available at http://lccn.loc.gov/2016944874

Contents

A Winning Team

The Cincinnati Bengals are a football team from Cincinnati, Ohio. They have played in the National Football League (NFL) for more than 45 years.

The Bengals have had good seasons and bad. But time and again, they've proven themselves. Let's see what makes the Bengals one of the NFL's greatest teams.

Black, orange, and white are the team's colors.

GRESHAM
84
65
BODINE
61
2

League Play

Team Standings

The AFC and the National Football Conference (NFC) make up the NFL. Each conference has a north, south, east, and west division.

The NFL got its start in 1920. Its teams have changed over the years. Today, there are 32 teams. They make up two conferences and eight divisions.

Fans get excited when major rivals face off!

The Bengals play in the North Division of the American Football Conference (AFC). This division also includes the Baltimore Ravens, the Cleveland Browns, and the Pittsburgh Steelers.

The Cleveland Browns are a major rival of the Bengals. Both teams are from Ohio.

Kicking Off

The Bengals were founded in 1967 by Paul Brown and a group of businessmen. The team began play in the American Football League (AFL) in 1968. In 1970, this league joined the NFL. The Bengals enjoyed early success.

Paul Brown Stadium was named after the team's founder (right). His son Mike Brown (left) is the team's current owner.

The Name Game

In 1968, Paul Brown nicknamed Cincinnati's AFL expansion franchise the Bengals. The name honored the football team that played in the city from 1937 to 1942.

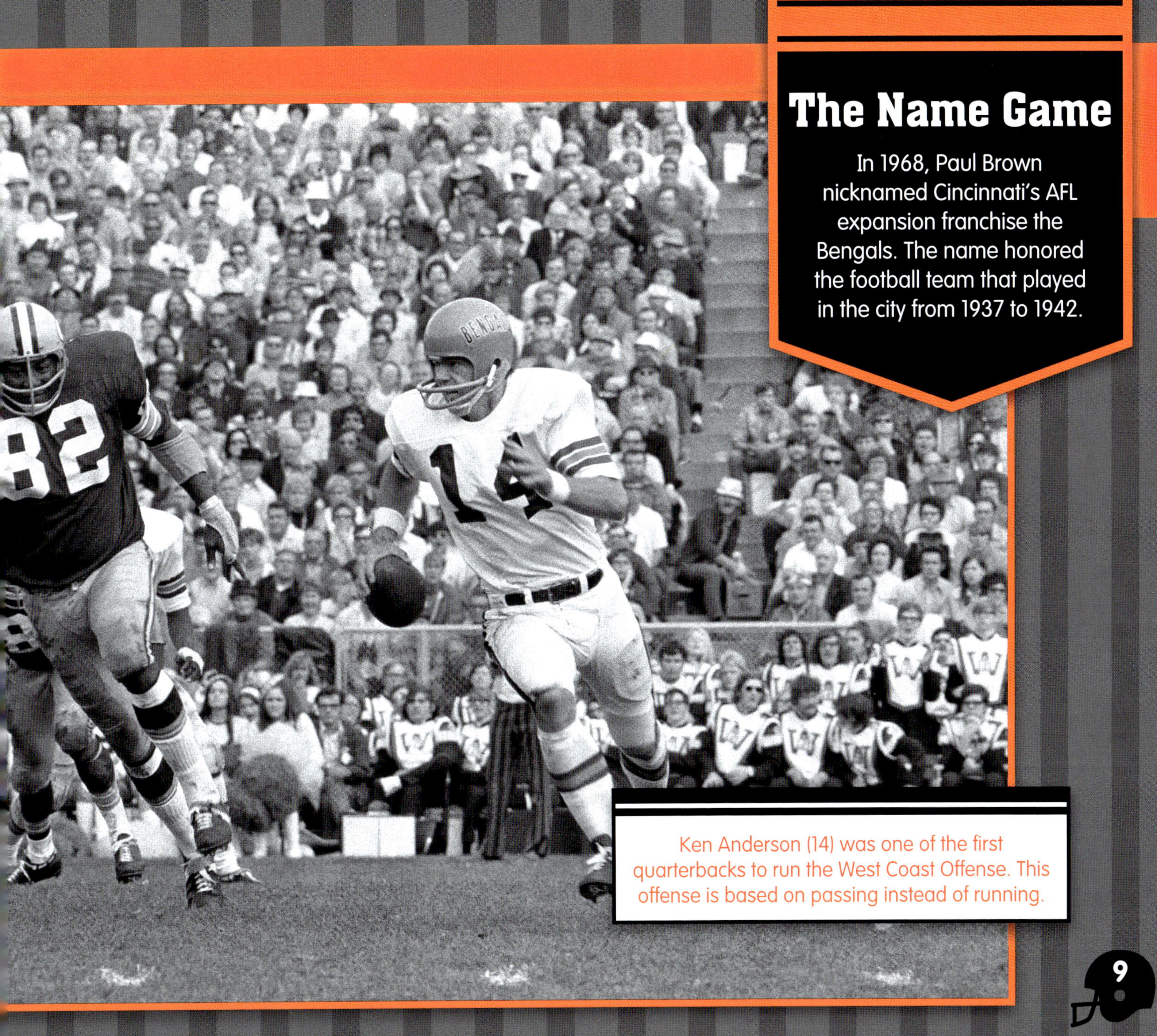

Ken Anderson (14) was one of the first quarterbacks to run the West Coast Offense. This offense is based on passing instead of running.

Highlight Reel

Win or Go Home

NFL teams play 16 regular season games each year. The teams with the best records are part of the play-off games. Play-off winners move on to the conference championships. Then, conference winners face off in the Super Bowl!

The Bengals won the AFC **championship** in 1981 and 1988. The team was excited to play in the Super Bowl. Sadly, they lost both times to the San Francisco 49ers.

From 1991 to 2004, the Bengals struggled. The team had losing records. It didn't make the play-offs. In 2005, the Bengals had their first winning season in 15 years. They also won the division title.

The Bengals beat the San Diego Chargers in one of the coldest games in history. The windchill made it feel like −9°F (−23°C).

As of 2016, Marvin Lewis is the longest-standing Bengals coach in history.

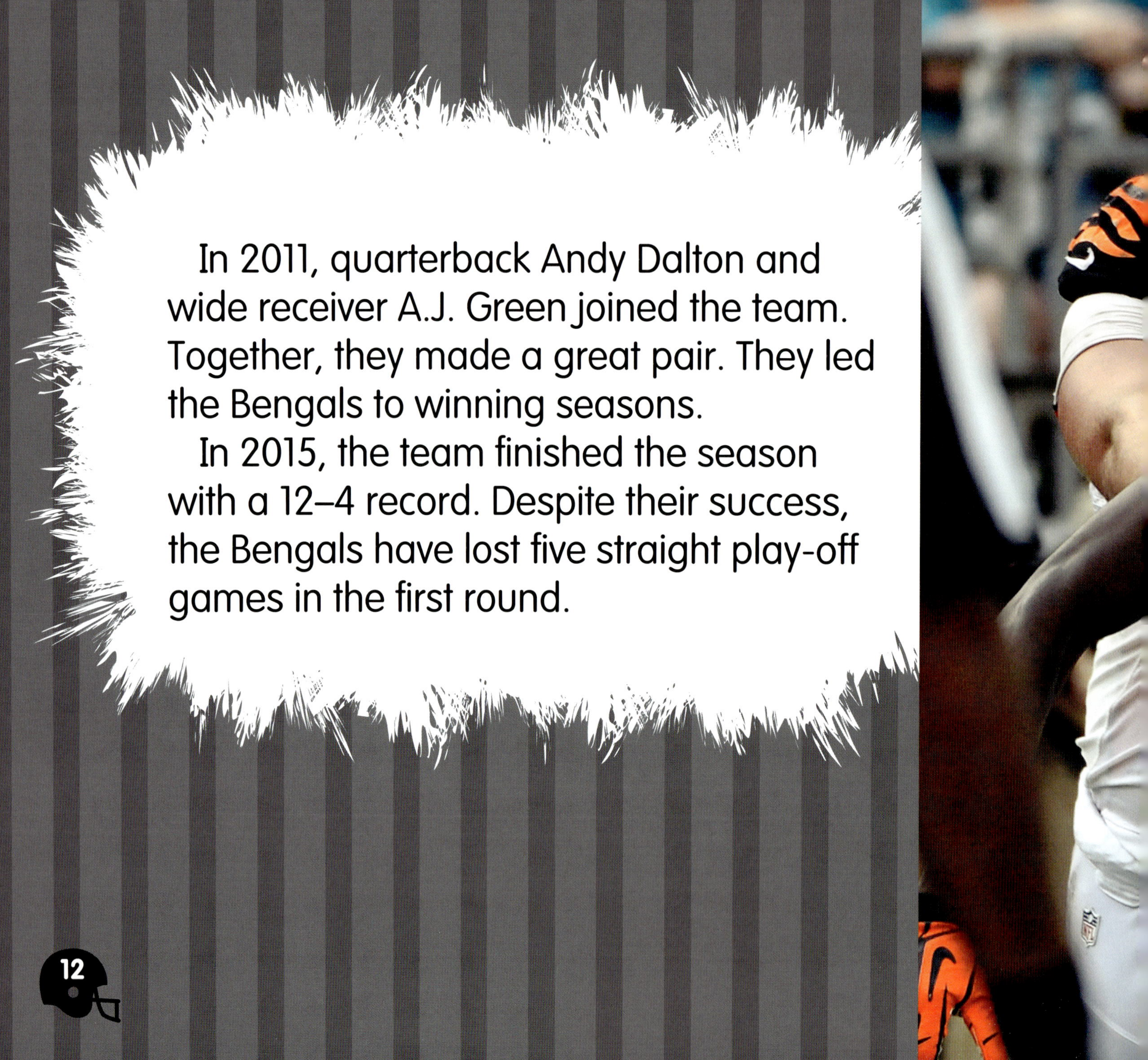

In 2011, quarterback Andy Dalton and wide receiver A.J. Green joined the team. Together, they made a great pair. They led the Bengals to winning seasons.

In 2015, the team finished the season with a 12–4 record. Despite their success, the Bengals have lost five straight play-off games in the first round.

A.J. Green (left) and Andy Dalton (right) are one of the NFL's greatest passing duos. They have led the team to five straight play-offs.

Halftime! Stat Break

Pro Football Hall of Famers & Their Years with the Bengals

Anthony Muñoz, Tackle (1980–1992)

Famous Coaches

Paul Brown (1968–1975)
Forrest Gregg (1980–1983)

Championships

SUPER BOWL APPEARANCES:
1982, 1989

SUPER BOWL WINS:
None

Team Records

RUSHING YARDS
Career: Corey Dillon, 8,061 yards (1997–2003)
Single Season: Rudi Johnson, 1,458 yards (2005)
PASSING YARDS
Career: Ken Anderson, 32,838 yards (1971–1986)
Single Season: Andy Dalton, 4,293 yards (2013)
RECEPTIONS
Career: Chad Johnson, 751 receptions (2001–2010)
Single Season: T.J. Houshmandzadeh, 112 receptions (2007)
ALL-TIME LEADING SCORER
Career: Jim Breech, 1,151 points (1980–1992)

Fan Fun

STADIUM: Paul Brown Stadium
LOCATION: Cincinnati, Ohio
MASCOT: Who Dey

Coaches' Corner

In 1968, founder Paul Brown became the Bengal's first head coach. Brown **drafted** key players and the team made it to the play-offs in 1970. Brown was named NFL Coach of the Year in 1969 and 1970. He **retired** from coaching in 1975.

Forrest Gregg was head coach of the Bengals from 1980 to 1983. Under his leadership, the team won 12 games in 1981. This set a Bengals record and earned the team a trip to its first Super Bowl!

Brown joined the Pro Football Hall of Fame before he coached the Bengals.

Gregg coached the first Bengals team that went to the play-offs for two straight seasons.

Star Players

Ken Riley DEFENSIVE BACK (1969–1983)

Ken Riley is famous for catching 65 **interceptions** throughout his **career**. This is a team record. Riley played with the Bengals for 15 seasons. He was in 207 games, which is another team record.

Ken Anderson QUARTERBACK (1971-1986)

Many people consider Ken Anderson to be the best Bengals quarterback in history. During his 12-year **career** with the team, Anderson set records and won **awards**. Anderson was named NFL Man of the Year in 1975 for his charity work. In 1981, he won the NFL Most Valuable Player (MVP) award.

Isaac Curtis WIDE RECEIVER (1973–1984)

Curtis was known for his speed. In his **rookie** season, he averaged 17.1 yards per catch. That is a team record! During his 12 years with the team, Curtis made 416 receptions for 7,101 yards and 53 touchdowns. He also played in two Super Bowls.

Anthony Muñoz TACKLE (1980–1992)

Anthony Muñoz is considered one of the best offensive linemen in history. He played for the Bengals his entire **career**. Muñoz was selected to play in the Pro Bowl, which is the NFL's all-star game, 11 straight years. In 1998, he became the first Bengals player in the Pro Football Hall of Fame.

Boomer Esiason QUARTERBACK (1984–1992, 1997)

The Bengals picked Boomer Esiason in the 1984 **draft**. Boomer, a left-handed quarterback, had his best season in 1988. He led the AFC in passing yards and helped his team make it to the Super Bowl. Boomer was also named the NFL MVP.

Andy Dalton QUARTERBACK (2011–)

In 2011, the Bengals chose Andy Dalton in the **draft**. In his **rookie** season, Dalton passed for more than 3,000 yards. Dalton also teamed up with running back A.J. Green to set many passing and receiving records. He is the only Bengals quarterback to catch a touchdown.

A.J. Green WIDE RECEIVER (2011–)

In 2011, A.J. Green was the team's fourth draft pick. The Bengals got a star player with Green. He is the only Bengals player invited to the Pro Bowl in each of his first five seasons. From 2011 to 2013, Green caught 260 passes. This set an NFL record.

Paul Brown Stadium

The Bengals play home games at Paul Brown Stadium. It is in Cincinnati. The stadium opened in 2000. It can hold more than 65,000 people.

From 1970 to 2000, the team played at Riverfront Stadium. They shared the space with baseball's Cincinnati Reds.

CINCINNATI
BENGALS
BENGALS
SALUTE TO SERVICE

Who Dey Bengals

Thousands of fans flock to Paul Brown Stadium to see the Bengals play home games. Fans love to **chant** "Who Dey!" to cheer the team.

The team's **mascot** is also named Who Dey. He entertains fans during home games.

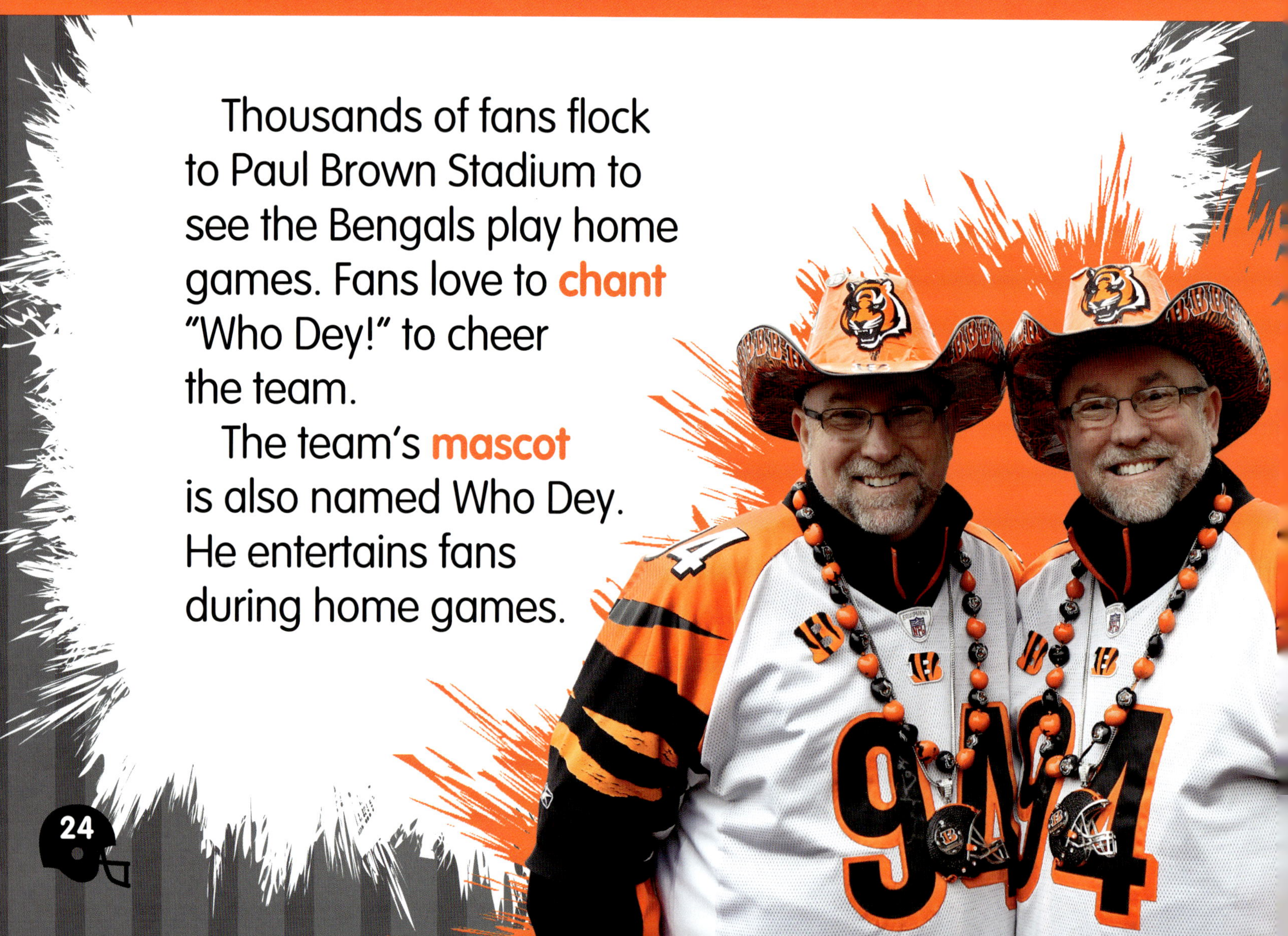

Who Dey stands on the sidelines during the national anthem.

Fans get excited to cheer on the Bengals!

Final Call

The Bengals have a long, rich history. They played in the Super Bowl in 1982 and 1989. But, they are still waiting for their first Super Bowl win.

Even during losing seasons, true fans have stuck by them. Many believe the Cincinnati Bengals will remain one of the greatest teams in the NFL.

Andy Dalton (14) celebrates with the team after scoring a touchdown.

Through the Years

1967

The team is founded by Paul Brown as part of the AFL.

1970

The AFL joins the NFL.

1972

Ken Anderson becomes the starting quarterback.

1981

The Bengals get new uniforms with tiger-striped helmets, jerseys, and pants.

1982

The Bengals play in their first Super Bowl. They lose to the San Francisco 49ers 26–21.

1989

The Bengals appear in their second Super Bowl. Again, they lose to the San Francisco 49ers.

2000

Paul Brown Stadium opens.

2003

Marvin Lewis is the team's new head coach.

2005

The Bengals win a division title.

2015

The Bengals make it to the play-offs for the fifth straight year.

Postgame Recap

1. When was the Bengals first playing season?
   A. 1967 **B**. 1968 **C**. 1969

2. What is the name of the stadium where the Bengals play home games?
   A. Ken Anderson Dome
   B. Paul Brown Stadium
   C. Boomer Esiason Stadium

3. Name the single Bengals player in the Pro Football Hall of Fame.

4. What is the name of the longest-standing Bengals coach?
   A. Forrest Gregg
   B. Bill Johnson
   C. Marvin Lewis

1. B. 2. B. 3. Anthony Muñoz 4. C.

Glossary

award something that is given in recognition of good work or a good act.

career a period of time spent in a certain job.

championship a game, a match, or a race held to find a first-place winner.

chant a word or phrase that is repeated to a beat. Usually, chants are spoken loudly by a crowd.

draft a system for professional sports teams to choose new players. When a team drafts a player, they choose that player for their team.

interception (ihn-tuhr-SEHP-shuhn) when a player catches a pass that was meant for the other team's player.

mascot something to bring good luck and help cheer on a team.

retire to give up one's job.

rookie a first-year player in a professional sport.

Websites

To learn more about the NFL's Greatest Teams, visit **booklinks.abdopublishing.com**. These links are routinely monitored and updated to provide the most current information available.

Index